THE
WORLD'S
BEST
PIANO

Arrangements

© 1991 CPP/Belwin, Inc.
15800 N.W. 48th Avenue, Miami, Florida 33014

Editor: Stuart Isacoff & Edward Shanaphy
Production: David C. Olsen

What Can I Say

AFTER I SAY I'M SORRY?

Piano Solo Arrangement by
ART TATUM

WALTER DONALDSON
ABE LYMAN

Moderate Swing Tempo

After I Say I'm Sorry - 2 - 1

AGAIN

Piano Interpretation by
GEORGE SHEARING

DORCAS COCHRAN
LIONEL NEWMAN

Again - 2 - 1

Again - 2 - 2

From the 20TH CENTURY-FOX Motion Picture "APRIL LOVE"

APRIL LOVE

Piano Interpretation by
GEORGE SHEARING

PAUL FRANCIS WEBSTER
SAMMY FAIN

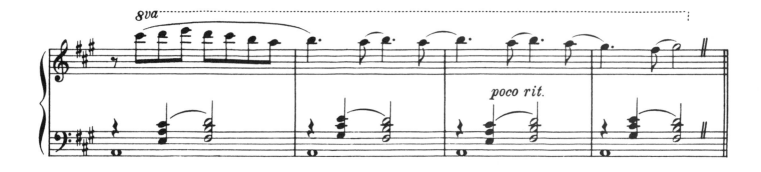

April Love - 2 - 1

9

April Love - 2 - 2

Theme from 20TH CENTURY-FOX Motion Picture "ANASTASIA"

ANASTASIA

Piano Interpretation by
GEORGE SHEARING

PAUL FRANCIS WEBSTER
ALFRED NEWMAN

Anastasia - 3 - 1

From the United Artists Motion Picture "HAIR"

AQUARIUS

Piano Interpretation by
GEORGE SHEARING

JAMES RADO
GEROME RAGNI
GALT MacDERMOT

Moderately

Aquarius - 5 - 1

To Coda

D.S. al Coda

Coda

rit.

a tempo

ARTISTRY IN RHYTHM

STAN KENTON

Artistry In Rhythm - 4 - 1

20

AT SUNDOWN

Piano Solo Arrangement by
ART TATUM

WALTER DONALDSON

Moderato

At Sundown - 2 - 1

A-TISKET A-TASKET

By ELLA FITZGERALD and
VAN ALEXANDER

A-Tisket A-Tasket - 2 - 1

AVALON TOWN

Piano Interpretation by
TEDDY WILSON

GRANT CLARKE
NACIO HERB BROWN

Avalon Town - 2 - 1

Avalon Town - 2 - 2

BLACK EYED SUSAN BROWN

Piano Solo Arranged by
THOMAS "FATS" WALLER

HERB MAGIDSON, AL HOFFMAN
and AL GOODHART

Black Eyed Susan Brown - 2 - 1

Black Eyed Susan Brown - 2 - 2

BLUE MOON

Piano Interpretation by
TEDDY WILSON

LORENZ HART
RICHARD RODGERS

Blue Moon - 2 - 1

BLUE RONDO A LA TURK

By DAVE BRUBECK

Blue Rondo A La Turk - 10 - 1

Blue Rondo A La Turk - 10 - 2

34

Blue Rondo A La Turk - 10 - 3

1st Improvisation

Blue Rondo A La Turk - 10 - 8

40

Blue Rondo A La Turk - 10 - 10

BY THE TIME I GET TO PHOENIX

Piano Interpretation by
GEORGE SHEARING

JIM WEBB

Moderately slow, with a steady beat

By The Time I Get To Phoenix - 4 - 1

By The Time I Get To Phoenix - 4 - 2

By The Time I Get To Phoenix - 4 - 4

C JAM BLUES

DUKE ELLINGTON

THE BOY NEXT DOOR

Words and Music by
HUGH MARTIN and
RALPH BLANE

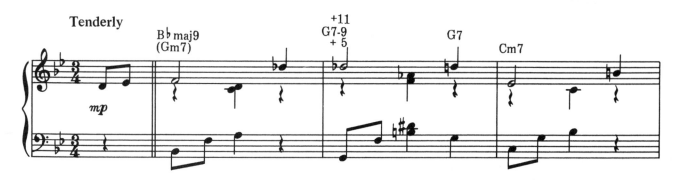

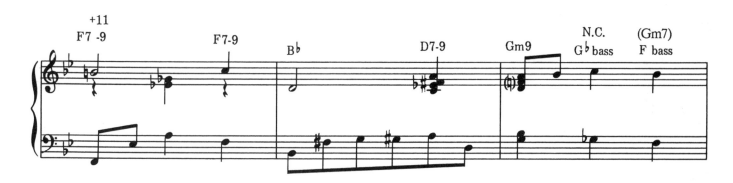

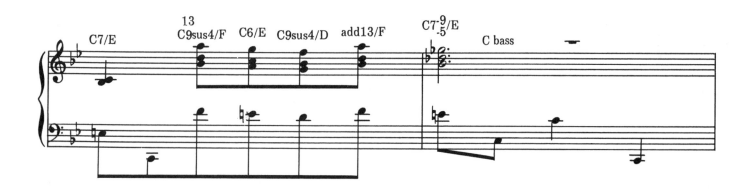

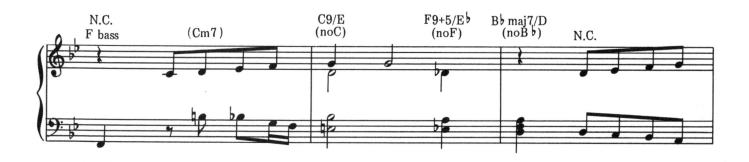

The Boy Next Door - 3 - 1

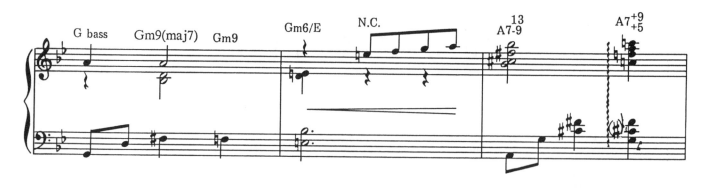

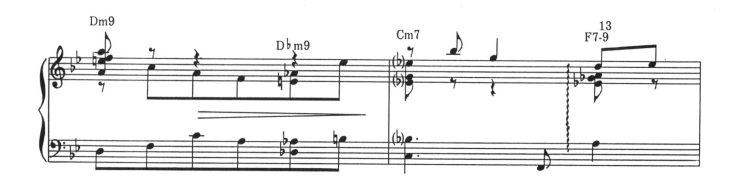

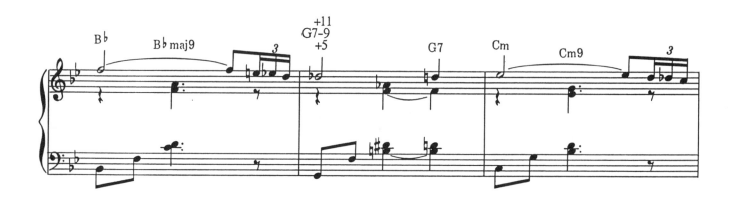

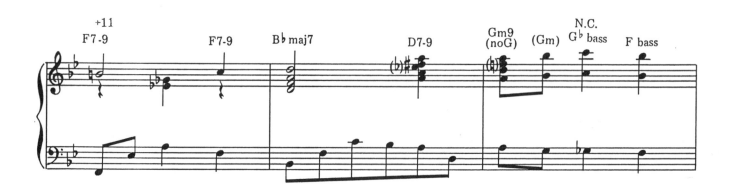

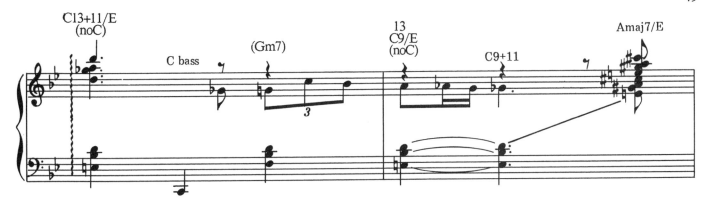

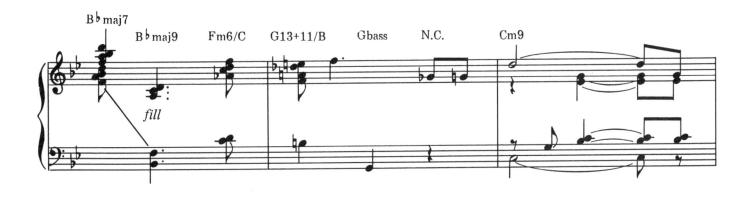

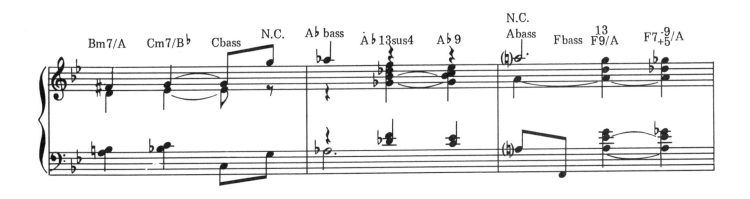

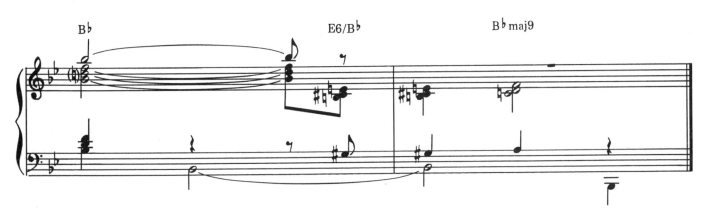

The Boy Next Door - 3 - 3

CABIN IN THE SKY

Piano Solo Arrangement by
EARL HINES

JOHN LATOUCHE
VERNON DUKE

Moderato

Cabin In The Sky - 2 - 1

CHARMAINE

Piano Interpretation by
GEORGE SHEARING

ERNO RAPEE
LEW POLLACK

Charmaine - 2 - 1

CHATTANOOGA CHOO CHOO

Piano Solo Arranged by
HAZEL SCOTT

Words by MACK GORDON
Music by HARRY WARREN

Chattanooga Choo Choo - 2 - 1

Chattanooga Choo Choo - 2 - 2

8va bassa . . . . !

CHINA BOY

Piano Interpretation by
FREDDIE SLACK

By DICK WINFREE and
PHIL BOUTELJE

China Boy - 2 - 1

China Boy - 2 - 2

THE DARKTOWN STRUTTERS' BALL

Piano Solo Arranged by
BOB ZURKE

By SHELTON BROOKS

The Darktown Strutter's Ball - 2 - 1

The Darktown Strutter's Ball - 2 - 2

59

DO NOTHIN''TILL YOU HEAR FROM ME

Piano Solo Arrangement by
EARL HINES

BOB RUSSELL
DUKE ELLINGTON

Moderately Slow

Do Nothin' 'Till You Hear From Me - 2 - 1

Do Nothin' 'Till You Hear From Me - 2 - 2

DOLL DANCE

from the "Hollywood Music Box Revue"
Capitol Record No. 113

Piano Interpretation by
FREDDIE SLACK

By NACIO HERB BROWN

Medium tempo

Doll Dance - 2 - 1

Doll Dance - 2 - 2

DON'T BE THAT WAY

Piano Arrangement by
EDDIE HEYWOOD

BENNY GOODMAN
EDGAR SAMPSON
MITCHELL PARISH

Don't Be That Way - 2 - 1

Don't Be That Way - 2 - 2

8 bassa

DON'T BLAME ME

Piano Interpretation by
GEORGE SHEARING

DOROTHY FIELDS
JIMMY McHUGH

Don't Blame Me - 2 - 1

DON'T GET AROUND MUCH ANYMORE

Piano Solo Arrangement by
EARL HINES

BOB RUSSELL
DUKE ELLINGTON

Don't Get Around Much Anymore - 2 - 1

Don't Get Around Much Anymore - 2 - 2

From the M-G-M Motion Picture "SWEET BIRD OF YOUTH"

EBB TIDE

Piano Interpretation by
GEORGE SHEARING

CARL SIGMAN
ROBERT MAXWELL

Ebb Tide - 3 - 1

EMILY

Piano Interpretation by
BILL EVANS

By
JOHNNY MERCER and
JOHNNY MANDEL

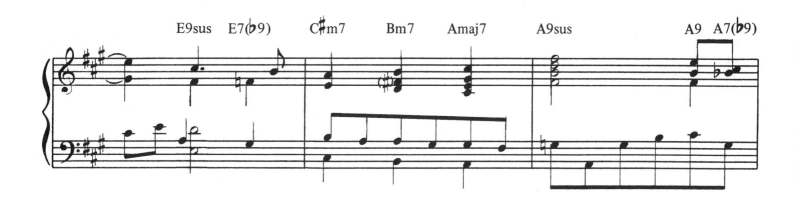

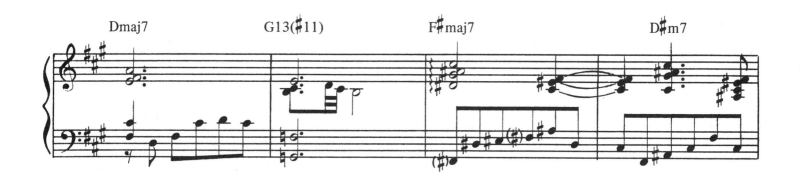

Emily - 11 - 1

Emily - 11 - 4

EVERYTHING I HAVE IS YOURS

Piano Interpretation by
GEORGE SHEARING

HAROLD ADAMSON
BURTON LANE

Everything I Have Is Yours - 2 - 1

Everything I Have Is Yours - 2 - 2

FIVE FOOT TWO, EYES OF BLUE

(Has Anybody Seen My Girl?)

Piano Solo Arranged by
HAZEL SCOTT

Words by SAM LEWIS and JOE YOUNG
Music by RAY HENDERSON

Bright tempo

Five Foot Two, Eyes Of Blue - 2 - 1

Five Foot Two, Eyes Of Blue - 2 - 2

FOR ALL WE KNOW

Piano Interpretation by
GEORGE SHEARING

SAM M. LEWIS
J. FRED COOTS

For All We Know - 2 - 1

For All We Know - 2 - 2

Recorded by GEORGE BENSON on CTI Records

THE GENTLE RAIN

Piano Interpretation by
GEORGE SHEARING

MATT DUBEY
LUIZ BONFA

The Gentle Rain - 2 - 1

The Gentle Rain - 2 - 2

GOOD NIGHT SWEETHEART

Piano Arrangement by
EDDIE HEYWOOD

RAY NOBLE
JIMMY CAMPBELL
REG. CONNELLY

Moderately bright

Good Night Sweetheart - 2 - 1

Good Night Sweetheart - 2 - 2

HOW ABOUT YOU

Piano Interpretation by
GEORGE SHEARING

By
RALPH FREED
and BURTON LANE

How About You - 2 - 1

How About You - 2 - 2

HOW AM I TO KNOW?

Piano Interpretation by
GEORGE SHEARING

DOROTHY PARKER
JACK KING

How Am I To Know - 2 - 1

How Am I To Know - 2 - 2

I CRIED FOR YOU

Piano Interpretation by
TEDDY WILSON

ARTHUR FREED
GUS ARNHEIM
ABE LYMAN

Medium Fox Trot

I Cried For You - 2 - 1

I Cried For You - 2 - 2

I GOT IT BAD AND THAT AIN'T GOOD

By
PAUL FRANCIS WEBSTER
and DUKE ELLINGTON

Piano Interpretation by
GEORGE SHEARING

Moderately Slow

I Got It Bad - 2 - 1

I Got It Bad - 2 - 2

IF I GIVE MY HEART TO YOU

Piano Interpretation by
GEORGE SHEARING

JIMMIE CRANE
AL JACOBS
JIMMY BREWSTER

Slowly

If I Give My Heart To You - 2 - 1

If I Give My Heart To You - 2 - 2

IF I HAD YOU

Piano Solo Arranged by
BOB ZURKE

By TED SHAPIRO, JIMMY CAMPBELL and
REG CONNELLY

If I Had You - 2 - 1

If I Had You - 2 - 2

I'LL NEVER BE THE SAME

Piano Solo Arrangement by
EARL HINES

GUS KAHN
MATT MALNECK
FRANK SIGNORELLI

Moderately slow

I'll Never Be The Same - 2 - 1

I'll Never Be The Same - 2 - 2

I'LL SEE YOU IN MY DREAMS

Piano Interpretation by
TEDDY WILSON

GUS KAHN
ISHAM JONES

Moderato

I'll See You In My Dreams - 2 - 1

I'M COMING VIRGINIA

Piano Solo Arranged by
MAURICE ROCCO

Words by WILL MARION COOK
Music by DONALD HEYWOOD

I'm Coming Virginia - 2 - 1

I'm Coming Virginia - 2 - 2

I'M IN THE MOOD FOR LOVE

Piano Arrangement by
EDDIE HEYWOOD

JIMMY McHUGH
DOROTHY FIELDS

I'm In The Mood For Love - 2 - 1

I'm In The Mood For Love - 2 - 2

I'M NOBODY'S BABY

Piano Solo Arranged by
THOMAS "FATS" WALLER

BENNY DAVIS, MILTON AGER
and LESTER SANTLY

I'm Nobody's Baby - 2 - 1

I'm Nobody's Baby - 2 - 2

I'M SITTING ON TOP OF THE WORLD

Piano Solo Arranged by
THOMAS "FATS" WALLER

LEWIS and YOUNG
and RAY HENDERSON

I'm Sitting On Top Of The World - 2 - 1

I'm Sitting On Top Of The World - 2 - 2

I'M THRU WITH LOVE

Piano Solo Arranged by
BOB ZURKE

Words by GUS KAHN
Music by MATT MALNECK and FUD LIVINGSTON

Medium tempo

I'm Thru With Love - 2 - 1

I'm Thru With Love - 2 - 2

I'M JUST A LUCKY SO-AND-SO

Piano Solo Arranged by
DUKE ELLINGTON

By
DUKE ELLINGTON and
MACK DAVID

I'm Just a Lucky So-and-So - 3 - 1

I'm Just a Lucky So-and-So - 3 - 2

Based on the Theme of the M-G-M Motion Picture "INVITATION"

INVITATION

Piano Interpretation by
GEORGE SHEARING

PAUL FRANCIS WEBSTER
BRONISLAU KAPER

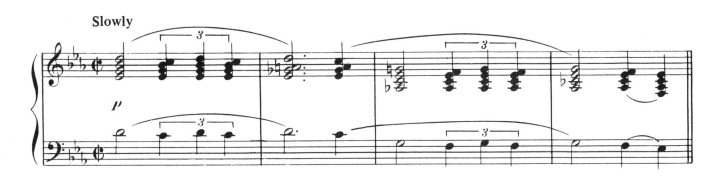

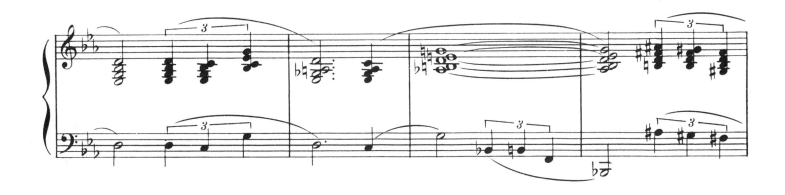

Invatation - 3 - 1

124

Invatation - 3 - 2

IN A MELLOW TONE

DUKE ELLINGTON

Medium Swing Tempo (*not too fast*)

In A Mellow Tone - 2 - 1

IN A MIST

Arranged by
MARY LOU WILLIAMS

BIX BEIDERBECKE

Moderately slow

In A Mist - 2 - 1

In A Mist - 2 - 2

IN YOUR OWN SWEET WAY

By
DAVE BRUBECK

Moderato (with a tender touch)

1st Improvisation

132

2nd Improvisation

3rd Improvisation

In Your Own Sweet Way - 8 - 8

IT DON'T MEAN A THING
(If It Ain't Got That Swing)

By
IR VING MILLS and
DUKE ELLINGTON

It Don't Mean A Thing - 2 - 1

It Don't Mean A Thing - 2 - 2

JA - DA

Piano Solo Arrangement by
ART TATUM

BOB CARLETON

Ja - Da - 2 - 1

THE JITTERBUG WALTZ

By
THOMAS "FATS" WALLER

The Jitterbug Waltz - 4 - 1

The Jitterbug Waltz - 4 - 2

JUST YOU, JUST ME

Piano Arrangement by
EDDIE HEYWOOD

RAYMOND KLAGES
JESSE GREER

Moderate swing tempo

Just You, Just Me - 2 - 1

Just You, Just Me - 2 - 2

SWEETIE, DEAR

Piano Solo Arrangement by
EARL HINES

WILL MARION COOK
JOE JORDAN

Bright

IT'S A RAGGY WALTZ

By
DAVE BRUBECK

It's A Raggy Waltz - 9 - 1

It's A Raggy Waltz - 9 - 3

2nd Improvisation

3rd Improvisation

It's A Raggy Waltz - 9 - 9

KATHY'S WALTZ

By
DAVE BRUBECK

Kathy's Waltz - 6 - 2

2nd Improvisation

3rd Improvisation

Kathy's Waltz - 6 - 5

KILLING ME SOFTLY WITH HIS SONG

Piano Interpretation by
GEORGE SHEARING

NORMAN GIMBEL
CHARLES FOX

Moderately

Killing Me Softly With His Song - 4 - 1

Killing Me Softly With His Song - 4 - 2

Killing Me Softly With His Song - 4 - 3

Killing Me Softly With His Song - 4 - 4

sostenuto ped.

From the 20th Century-Fox Motion Picture "LAURA"

LAURA

Arranged by
GEORGE SHEARING

JOHNNY MERCER
DAVID RAKSIN

Laura - 2 - 1

Laura - 2 - 2

Recorded by MARGO SMITH on WARNER BROS. Records

LITTLE THINGS MEAN A LOT

Piano Interpretation by
GEORGE SHEARING

EDITH LINDEMAN
CARL STUTZ

Slowly, with expression

Little Things Mean a Lot - 2 - 1

rit.   a tempo   poco   accel e   dim.   pp

Little Things Mean A Lot - 2 - 2

Ped.   *

From the 20th Century-Fox Motion Picture "LOVE IS A MANY-SPLENDORED THING"

LOVE IS A MANY-SPLENDORED THING

Piano Interpretation by
GEORGE SHEARING

PAUL FRANCIS WEBSTER
SAMMY FAIN

Love Is A Many - Splendored Thing - 2 - 1

poco rit.

poco rit.   *f*   *mf*   *slower*   *allarg.*

p

Love Is A Many - Splendored Thing - 2 - 2

LULLABY IN RHYTHM

Piano Solo Arrangement by
MARY LOU WILLIAMS

BENNY GOODMAN
EDGAR SAMPSON
CLARENCE PROFIT
WALTER HIRSCH

Lullaby In Rhythm - 2 - 1

Lullaby In Rhythm - 2 - 2

MARGIE

Piano Solo Arranged by
THOMAS "FATS" WALLER

By
BENNY DAVIS, CON CONRAD
and J. RUSSELL ROBINSON

Margie - 2 - 1

from the M-G-M picture "Montana Moon"

THE MOON IS LOW

Piano Solo Arrangement by
ART TATUM

ARTHUR FREED
NACIO HERB BROWN

The Moon Is Low - 2 - 1

179

The Moon Is Low - 2 - 2

Recorded by *BOBBY VINTON* on ABC Records

MOONLIGHT SERENADE

Piano Interpretation by
GEORGE SHEARING

By
MITCHELL PARISH and
GLENN MILLER

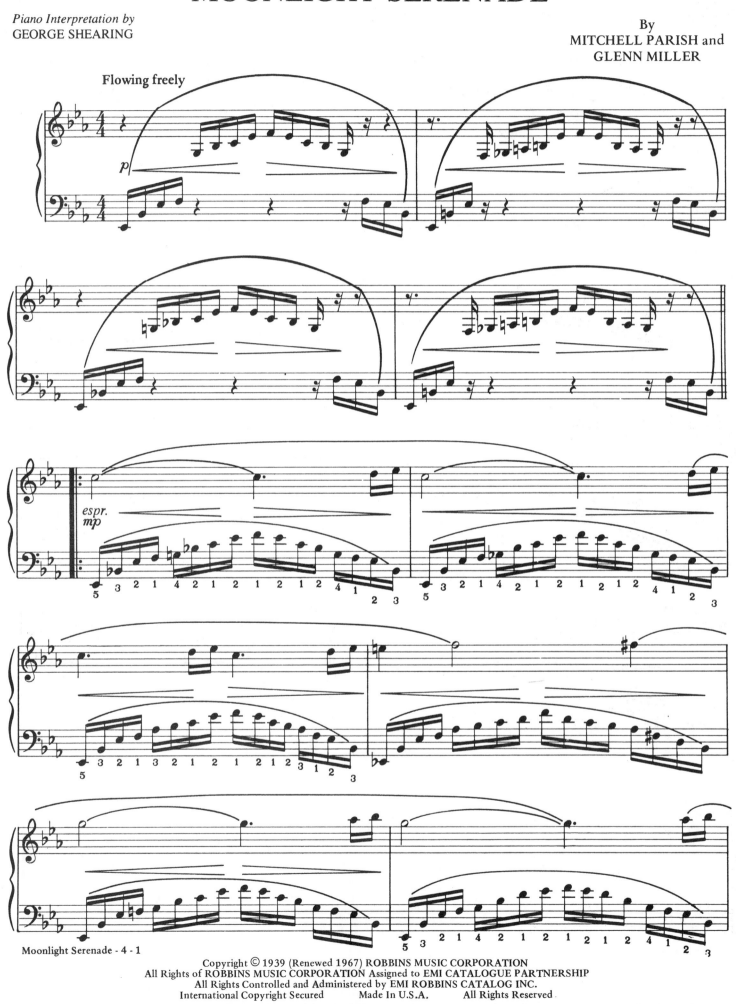

Moonlight Serenade - 4 - 1

poco mosso

Moonlight Serenade - 4 - 2

Tempo I

MY BLUE HEAVEN

Piano Interpretation by
TEDDY WILSON

GEORGE WHITING
WALTER DONALDSON

My Blue Heaven - 2 - 1

My Blue Heaven - 2 - 2

MOOD INDIGO

By
DUKE ELLINGTON, IRVING MILLS
and ALBANY BIGARD

ON GREEN DOLPHIN STREET

Piano Interpretation by
GEORGE SHEARING

By
NED WASHINGTON and
BRONISLAU KAPER

Moderately bright

On Green Dolphin Street - 3 - 1

On Green Dolphin Street - 3 - 3

ONCE IN A WHILE

Piano Interpretation by
GEORGE SHEARING

BUD GREEN
MICHAEL EDWARDS

Once In A While - 2 - 1

Once In A While - 2 - 2

ONE O'CLOCK JUMP

Arranged by
BOB ZURKE

COUNT BASIE

One O'Clock Jump - 6 - 1

One O'Clock Jump - 6 - 4

198

One O'Clock Jump - 6 - 5

One O'Clock Jump - 6 - 6

From the M-G-M Picture "THE WIZARD OF OZ"

OVER THE RAINBOW

Arranged by
GEORGE SHEARING

E.Y. HARBURG
HAROLD ARLEN

Over The Rainbow - 2 - 1

PAGAN LOVE SONG

Piano Interpretation by
TEDDY WILSON

ARTHUR FREED
NACIO HERB BROWN

Pagan Love Song - 2 - 1

PENNSYLVANIA 6-5000

Piano Solo Arranged by
THOMAS "FATS" WALLER

CARL SIGMAN and
JERRY GRAY

Pennsylvania 6-5000 - 2 - 1

ROSE ROOM

Piano Interpretation by
TEDDY WILSON

HARRY WILLIAMS
ART HICKMAN

Medium Fox Trot

Rose Room - 2 - 1

Rose Room - 2 - 2

SATIN DOLL

Music by
DUKE ELLINGTON

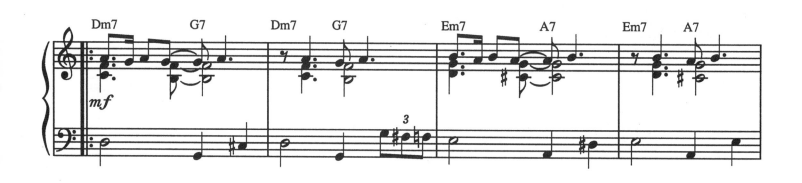

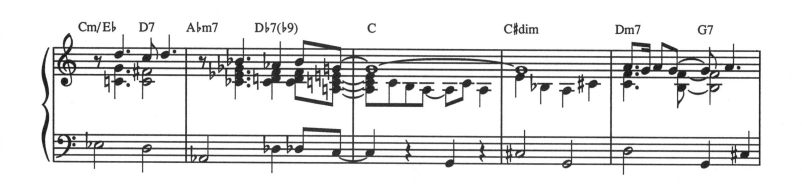

Satin Doll - 2 - 1

209

Satin Doll - 2 - 2

SHOULD I

Piano Interpretation by
GEORGE SHEARING

ARTHUR FREED
NACIO HERB BROWN

Should I - 3 - 1

SING, SING, SING
(With A Swing)

LOUIS PRIMA
Arranged by JESS STACY

*All small notes are to be played PP

Sing, Sing, Sing - 7 - 1

214

SLEEPY TIME GAL

JOS. R. ALDEN
RAYMOND B. EGAN
ANGE LORENZO
RICHARD A. WHITING

Arranged by
MARY LOU WILLIAMS
Fast tempo

Sleepy Time Gal - 2 - 1

Sleepy Time Gal - 2 - 2

SO RARE

Piano Interpretation by
GEORGE SHEARING

By
JACK SHARPE
and JERRY HERST

So Rare - 2 - 1

From the Musical Comedy "I MARRIED AN ANGEL"

SPRING IS HERE

Piano Interpretation by
GEORGE SHEARING

LORENZ HART
RICHARD RODGERS

Spring Is Here - 2 - 1

STOMPIN' AT THE SAVOY

Piano Solo Arrangement by
EDDIE HEYWOOD

BENNY GOODMAN
CHICK WEBB
EDGAR SAMPSON

Stompin' At The Savoy - 2 - 1

Stompin' At The Savoy - 2 - 2

8bassa

SOPHISTICATED LADY

Piano Solo Arranged by
DUKE ELLINGTON

By
IRVING MILLS, MITCHELL PARISH
and DUKE ELLINGTON

Moderato

Sophisticated Lady - 3 - 1

230

STORMY WEATHER
(Keeps Rainin' All The Time)

Words by
TED KOHLER

Music by
HAROLD ARLEN
Arranged by ED SHANAPHY

Stormy Weather - 3 - 1

232

Stormy Weather - 3 - 2

STUMBLING

Piano Interpretation by
TEDDY WILSON

ZEZ CONFREY

Stumbling - 2 - 1

Stumbling - 2 - 2

SWEET AND LOVELY

Piano Interpretation by
TEDDY WILSON

GUS ARNHEIM
HARRY TOBIAS
JULES LEMARE

Sweet And Lovely - 2 - 1

Sweet And Lovely - 2 - 2

8 bassa

SWEET LORRAINE

Words by
MITCHELL PARISH

Music by
CLIFF BURWELL
Arranged by ED SHANAPHY

Sweet Lorraine - 3 - 1

Sweet Lorraine - 3 - 2

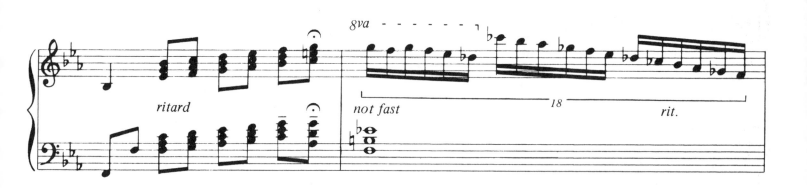

From the M-G-M Motion Picture "GOING HOLLYWOOD"

TEMPTATION

Piano Interpretation by
GEORGE SHEARING

ARTHUR FREED
NACIO HERB BROWN

Moderately (with feeling)

Temptation - 3 - 1

TAKE FIVE

By
PAUL DESMOND

Take Five - 4 - 1

Take Five - 4 - 2

246

Take Five - 4 - 3

Take Five - 4 - 4

TAKING A CHANCE ON LOVE

Piano Solo Arrangement by
EARL HINES

JOHN LATOUCHE
TED FETTER
VERNON DUKE

Moderate swing tempo

Taking A Chance On Love - 2 - 1

Taking A Chance On Love - 2 - 2

8 bassa

TRY A LITTLE TENDERNESS

Piano Interpretation by
GEORGE SHEARING

HARRY WOODS
JIMMY CAMPBELL
REG CONNELLY

Try A Little Tendernesss - 2 - 1

Try A Little Tenderness - 2 - 2

TWO SLEEPY PEOPLE

Piano Interpretation by
"FATS" WALLER

Words by FRANK LOESSER
Music by HOAGY CARMICHAEL

Moderately slow

254

From the United Artists Motion Picture "THE HAPPY ENDING"

WHAT ARE YOU DOING THE REST OF YOUR LIFE?

Piano Interpretation by
GEORGE SHEARING

By
ALAN and MARILYN BERGMAN
and MICHEL LEGRAND

Slowly (freely, with expression)

What Are You Doing The Rest Of Your Life? - 3 - 2

What Are You Doing The Rest Of Your Life? - 3 - 3

WABASH BLUES

Piano Solo Arrangement by
ART TATUM

DAVE RINGLE
FRED MEINKEN

from the M-G-M picture "The Night Is Young"

WHEN I GROW TOO OLD TO DREAM

Piano Solo Arrangement by
ART TATUM

OSCAR HAMMERSTEIN II
SIGMUND ROMBERG

When I Grow Too Old To Dream - 2 - 1

WHEN YOU WORE A TULIP
(And I Wore A Big Red Rose)

Piano Interpretation by
TEDDY WILSON

JACK MAHONEY
PERCY WENRICH

When You Wore A Tulip - 2 - 2

WHISPERING

Piano Solo Arranged by
MAURICE ROCCO

Words and Music by
JOHN SCHONBERGER, RICHARD COBURN
and VINCENT ROSE

Bright tempo

Whispering - 2 - 1

Whispering - 2 - 2

WHO'S SORRY NOW?

Piano Solo Arranged by
THOMAS "FATS" WALLER

By
BERT KALMAR, HARRY RUBY
and **TED SNYDER**

Who's Sorry Now? - 2 - 1

YOU ARE MY LUCKY STAR

Boogie Woogie Arr. by
DUKE ELLINGTON

ARTHUR FREED
NACIO HERB BROWN

You Are My Lucky Star - 2 - 1

You Are My Lucky Star - 2 - 2

YOU SHOWED ME THE WAY

Piano Solo Arrangement by
EARL HINES

BUD GREEN
ELLA FITZGERALD
TEDDY McCRAE
CHICK WEBB

You Showed Me The Way - 2 - 1

You Showed Me The Way - 2 - 2

YOU WERE MEANT FOR ME

Piano Interpretation by
GEORGE SHEARING

ARTHUR FREED
NACIO HERB BROWN

You Were Meant For Me - 2 - 1

WHAT IS A 'FAKE' MUSIC BOOK?

(For Starters, It Has Over 1000 Songs In It!)

IT'S THE ONE BOOK EVERY MUSICIAN, PROFESSIONAL OR AMATEUR, MUST OWN.
IT'S WHAT PRO MUSICIANS CALL <u>THE BIBLE</u>.

Here are just some of the **1010** songs you get . . .

It contains every kind of song for every kind of occasion. Hit songs of today such as **Don't It Make My Brown Eyes Blue** . . . great standards like **I'll See You In My Dreams** . . . show tunes like **Tomorrow!** . . . songs of the Roaring 20's such as **Five Foot Two!** . . . Irish songs, folk songs, Italian songs, Hawaiian songs, great classical themes, sacred songs, rock n' roll songs, Christmas songs, movie songs, Latin songs, patriotic songs, waltzes, marches, you name it! *It is the one songbook meant to fill every request.*

CHOCK FULL OF HITS It has four pounds, almost 500 pages, of *solid music* . . . with all the lyrics, melodies, and chord names. It contains a complete alphabetical listing *plus* a cross-reference listing by song category for the immediate location of any song. It is handsomely spiral bound so that it lies perfectly flat on your music stand, and has a durable leatherette textured cover. It was built to last through years of use.

A MUSICIAN'S DREAM COME TRUE Until recently, such books, if you could find them, were sold "under the table." And musicians would pay a great amount. But now we can *legally* bring you what those same musicians are calling the *greatest* fake book of them all . . . **The Legit Professional Fake Book.**

MONEY BACK GUARANTEE TOO! If you do not agree that this book is everything we say it is and more . . . if you are not completely thrilled and delighted for any reason whatsoever, simply return it to us within 30 days (it will take you a *full* 30 days just to get through it!), and we will send you a *complete* refund. When you think of all this music, 1010 great songs, *at less than 3¢ a song,* songs which sell for up to $2.00 each in stores, you realize what a great bargain this book is for just $35. It is a book which you will use and cherish over and over again in years to come, whether it's party time, or Christmas time, or just by yourself time at the piano.

A GREAT GIFT IDEA! If you are not a musician yourself, don't you know someone who would really love to have this book? It is truly a gift for all seasons.

Because you bought this book ...
Here's a
Money-Saving Offer

Sheet Music Magazine *brings you the songs you love to play*

We print lots of songs, *right in our magazine,* that are the most popular, best-loved songs ever written. And we don't just print the words. You get all the music too, with full sheet music arrangements ... PLUS ... lots of great tips and lessons from the pros to get you playing your best. In fact, there's an entire **music workshop** section in each issue which is used by thousands of music teachers and their students nationwide.

Above all, **Sheet Music Magazine** is a music magazine for amateur at-home musicians who just like to relax and have fun with their music. When your first issue arrives in the mail, we guarantee you'll drop everything and head to your piano or guitar, or maybe you'll just start singing right there by the mailbox. You get at least a dozen songs with each and every issue. And what great songs they are. The exciting songs of today, the golden hits of yesteryear. The love songs. The fun songs. The somebody done somebody wrong songs. It's the perfect answer for a good old fashioned sing-along party too.

Now Save 10%!

Let us send you your first jumbo, jam-packed issue with no obligation whatsoever. If you decide to cancel we'll send you your money back, and you may keep the special first issue as our gift. And that will end the matter. That's our way of saying thanks for giving us a try. If you do keep your subscription — or if you already subscribe and want to renew — we'll take 10% off our regular price of $15.97 as a special gift for purchasing this book! You pay just $14.37.

So order TODAY. You have absolutely nothing to lose *... and lots of good music in store!*

Sheet Music Magazine ... the world's most popular music magazine.

Here are 20 Great Songs included in your first issue of Sheet Music Magazine ...
Evergreen • Together • As Time Goes By • A Time For Love • Somewhere My Love • After The Lovin' • Morning Has Broken • Three Little Words • It Had To Be You • The Sound of Silence • Rose Garden • Chattanooga Choo Choo • Crying • Misty • Born To Lose • From A Distance • Tennessee Waltz • It All Depends On You • I've Got A Crush On You
This offer is our way of introducing this exciting song magazine to people who love to play music.